# JEWISH IMMIGRANTS

## 1880-1924

by Susan E. Haberle

Content Consultant:
Julie Koven, Reference/Cataloging Librarian
American Jewish Historical Society
New York, New York

## Blue Earth Books

an imprint of Capstone Press
Mankato, Minnesota

Blue Earth Books are published by Capstone Press
151 Good Counsel Drive, P.O. Box 669, Mankato, Minnesota 56002
http://www.capstone-press.com

*Library of Congress Cataloging-in-Publication Data*
Haberle, Susan E.
    Jewish Immigrants, 1880–1924 / by Susan E. Haberle.
      p. cm. — (Coming to America)
    Summary: Discusses reasons why Jewish people left their homelands to come to America, the experiences immigrants had in the new
    country, and contributions they made to American society.
    Includes bibliographical references and index.
    ISBN 0-7368-1207-5 (hardcover)
      1. Jews—United States—History—Juvenile literature. 2. Immigrants—United States—History—Juvenile literature. 3. Jews—Europe—Migrations—
Juvenile literature. 4. United States—Emigration and immigration—Juvenile literature. 5. Europe—Emigration and immigration—Juvenile literature.
[1. Jews—United States—History. 2. Immigrants—History. 3. Jews—Migrations. 4. United States—Emigration and immigration—History. 5. Europe—
Emigration and immigration—History.] I. Title II. Coming to America (Mankato, Minn.)
    E184.35 .H23 2003
    973' .04924—dc21                                                                                      2002000892

**Editorial credits**
Editor: Katy Kudela
Series Designer: Heather Kindseth
Book Designer: Jennifer Schonborn
Photo Researcher: Stacy Foster
Product Planning Editor: Karen Risch

**Photo credits**
Hulton/Archive Photos, cover, 9, 10, 11, 12, 16; Gregg Andersen, flag
images throughout; Bettmann/CORBIS, 4, 7, 13, 21; CORBIS, 8, 17,
19, 20, 22, 23; Capstone Press/Gary Sundermeyer, 15, 25; Minnesota
Historical Society, 18; FPG International LLC, 24; Roger Ressmeyer/
CORBIS, 26; Al Bello/AllSport, 29 (top); AFP/CORBIS, 29
(bottom)

1 2 3 4 5 6 07 06 05 04 03 02

# Contents

Chapter 1—Early Jewish Immigrants     4

Chapter 2—Life in the Old Country     8

Chapter 3—The Trip Over     12

Chapter 4—Arriving in America     16

Chapter 5—Surviving in America     20

Chapter 6—Keeping Traditions     24

Features

Immigration Route Map     5

Make a Family Tree     27

Timeline     28

Famous Jewish Americans     29

Words to Know     30

To Learn More     31

Places to Write and Visit     31

Internet Sites     32

Index     32

# EARLY JEWISH IMMIGRANTS

*Many Jewish immigrants came to America in search of a better life. They wanted to earn money and freely practice their religion.*

I n the late 1800s, Jewish immigrants came to America from many European countries. Jewish people did not have a homeland until the country of Israel formed in 1948. Jews are people who follow the Jewish religion or have Jewish ancestors.

The Jewish religion is about 3,500 years old. According to the Bible, Moses led the Jews out of slavery in Egypt to the land of Canaan, later called Palestine. About 2,000 years ago, Jews were forced to leave Canaan to find homes in other countries. Many Jews went to Europe.

The first Jewish immigrants came to America from Brazil. In 1654, Jews aboard the *Sainte Catherine* emigrated from Brazil. These 23 Jews settled in the Dutch colony of New Amsterdam, which later became New York City.

By 1776, there were 2,500 Jewish settlers in the 13 American colonies. Many Jewish immigrants settled in Philadelphia in

# Immigration Route

ENGLAND

RUSSIA

POLAND

HUNGARY

GERMANY

AUSTRIA

ROMANIA

New York City

UNITED
STATES

Atlantic
Ocean

N

W        E

S

Liverpool

Hamburg

Warsaw

RUSSIA

ENGLAND

GERMANY

POLAND

Kiev

HUNGARY

Vienna

AUSTRIA

ROMANIA

The journey for some Jews began by boarding trains in cities including Kiev in Russia, or Warsaw in Poland. These immigrants traveled to seaport cities where they joined other Jewish immigrants bound for America. Many Jews came to the ocean seaport city of Liverpool in England. Others traveled to cities located near major rivers. These cities included Vienna in Austria, Hamburg in Germany, and Warsaw in Poland.

5

Pennsylvania, Savannah in Georgia, Newport in Rhode Island, Charleston in South Carolina, or New York City.

Two large groups of Jewish immigrants came to America between 1820 and 1920. The first group of Jewish people came from Germany, Austria, and Hungary. These immigrants left to seek a better life. They were tired of the limits the government placed on them. They wanted to be treated fairly. The first group of Jewish immigrants were sometimes called German Jews. About 400,000 German Jews came to America between 1820 and 1880.

The greatest number of Jewish immigrants came to America between 1880 and 1920. These immigrants came from Poland, Russia, Romania, and other eastern European countries. This second group of Jewish immigrants wanted freedom to practice their religion. From 1880 to 1920, more than 2 million Jews immigrated from Eastern Europe to the United States.

Most Jewish immigrants arrived in New York City. Many settled in cities along the East Coast. Today, most Jewish Americans are descendants from this second wave.

In 1924, the U.S. Congress set limits on the number of immigrants who were allowed entry into America. Jewish immigration slowed down. Today, there are about 6 million Jewish Americans in the United States. Jews continue to immigrate to America for job opportunities and religious freedom.

*Many Jewish immigrants came to America with their extended families. After 1920, Jewish immigrants continued coming to America.*

# LIFE IN THE OLD COUNTRY

*Jewish men and boys spent much of their time studying religion.*

Although Jewish immigrants came from different countries, they had many things in common. Their strong religious faith was more than a religion. Judaism was a way of life. Jewish people celebrated the Sabbath, known as the Shabbat, from sunset on Friday to sunset on Saturday. During Shabbat, the Jews did not work. They gathered as families to worship in synagogues.

Jewish parents placed a great deal of importance on education. In the Jewish home, the father earned a living and studied religion. The mother cared for the children and the house. Men and boys studied religion, Hebrew, the Bible, and Jewish law. In Russia, Jewish girls were not allowed to go to school, but they did study at home.

The Jewish religion required special preparation of meals. Food that is prepared or eaten based on these laws is called kosher food. Jewish people can eat meat from animals such as cattle or sheep, but religious law forbids eating meat from pigs. Seafood with gills and scales is allowed, but not shellfish such as shrimp or crabs. Milk and meat are not served at the same meal.

During the early 1800s, Jews in Germany were able to buy land and live wherever they chose. They also served in the army. But German Jews were treated differently because of their religion. German Jews were barred from holding most public offices. Although their children were able to attend state schools, Jewish adults could not work at state-supported universities.

8

*Russian Jews were saddened by the move to the Pale of Settlement. In 1790, the Russian government ordered Jews to live in this area. The Pale of Settlement was located in southwest Russia.*

The German Jews began turning away from the traditional Jewish life to fit better into society. They began to question their traditions and language. Jews in Germany spoke Hebrew for prayers, Yiddish for daily conversation with other Jews, and German for conversation with other Germans. Soon many German Jews stopped speaking Yiddish and spoke only German.

During the late 1700s, Jewish people in Russia and Poland began to experience social discrimination called anti-Semitism. Jews were heavily taxed and not allowed to vote. The rulers in Russia and Poland wanted Jews to change their religious faith from Judaism to Christianity.

In 1790, the Russian government set up an area of land called the Pale of Settlement to keep Jewish people together. The Pale of Settlement was a territory in southwest Russia that was about twice the size of the state of California. By 1900, about 5 million Jews lived in the Pale of Settlement. They were not allowed to live in cities

*Many Jewish men learned the skills of a tailor. Jewish tailor shops continued to grow throughout the 1900s.*

within the territory. Instead they lived in all-Jewish towns and villages called shtetls.

Russian Jews also were forced to find new employment. They were not allowed to own land, so they could not work as farmers. Some Russian Jews became peddlers. Others worked as bankers, cobblers, and butchers. Some Russian Jews worked on railroads or rivers.

Many men became tailors. Jewish law did not allow Jews to wear clothes made of both wool and linen. Many Jews from eastern Europe only wore clothes made by Jewish tailors.

Although Russian Jews adapted to their new surroundings in the Pale of Settlement, they continued to live in fear. Under the rule of Russia's Tsar Nicholas I (1825–1855), boys were drafted into the Russian army at age 9. In 1881, a member of a radical group killed Russia's Tsar Alexander II. Many Russian Christians believed the Jews helped to plan this assassination. Angered by this death, Russian soldiers began attacking Jewish villages. During these attacks, called pogroms, soldiers killed Jews and destroyed their villages.

Stories of a better life in America began to spread through Jewish communities. Jews saw America as a Goldineh Medineh, or golden land, where they could live in peace. The Jews who stayed behind continued to suffer from the hatred of others. These feelings of hatred led to the Holocaust that took place during World War II (1939–1945). Under the leadership of Germany's leader, Adolf Hitler, the German Nazi party killed 6 million Jews. This tragedy has become known as the Holocaust.

# ★ Jews Suffer From Hatred ★

Following World War I (1914–1918), Germany suffered from economic troubles. Many German citizens were left without jobs. But German Jews were largely successful business people, especially in the area of finance.

Many German citizens were angry and jealous of the success earned by the German Jews. Among those who held a strong hatred toward the Jews was Adolf Hitler, leader of the German Nazi party. Hitler blamed all of Germany's problems on the Jews.

In 1933, the Nazi party came to power in Germany. The Nazis believed that the Germans were a superior race. They also believed Jews were not worthy of living.

By 1938, German Jews were sent to concentration camps. Many Jews were tortured. Some Jews were used as slave labor or for medical experiments.

During World War II (1939–1945), the Nazis killed more than 6 million European Jews in concentration camps. A Holocaust Memorial Museum was created in 1993 in Washington, D.C., to honor those who died in the Holocaust.

*Nazi soldiers posted signs on Jewish storefronts. The signs encouraged Germans to avoid Jewish shops.*

# THE TRIP OVER

*During good weather, seasick passengers often tried to get a little fresh air on the deck of the ship. Most immigrants traveled in the steerage section in the lowest part of the ship. Steerage was the least expensive way to travel.*

M any German Jewish immigrants were men who came to the United States to earn a better living. Unmarried single men hoped to start a new life in America. Married men hoped to earn a better income so they could bring their families to America.

Many German Jews joined family members who were already in America. One brother would bring others over to join his peddling business. Brothers encouraged their sisters to immigrate to work, keep house, or find a husband.

Before the 1880s, Jewish immigrants traveled to the United States in sailing ships. Many immigrants used their life savings to pay for the trip. The voyage to America usually took 90 days.

After 1881, Jewish immigrants began traveling in steamships. This faster form of travel took about 45 days to reach America. By 1900, ship travel improved so much that a trip across the Atlantic Ocean took six days. In 1903, a steamship ticket cost $34, a sum that took many years for a person to save.

When they saw the Statue of Liberty, immigrants knew
they had arrived in America.

"When we were told, on a Saturday
morning, we would be passing the
Statue of Liberty, we all lined the
deck. The thrill of seeing that statue
there. And the tears in everybody's
eyes, which, as a child, got me the
same feeling. It was more, not
freedom from oppression, I think,
but more freedom from want."

—Larry Edelman, immigrated
in 1920 at age 10

Most immigrants from Eastern Europe first traveled to seaports. Eastern European Jews relied on major port cities such as Vienna in Austria, Hamburg in Germany, or Liverpool in England.

Many Russian Jewish families arrived in America together. Russian Jews immigrated with extended family members including aunts, uncles, and cousins. The journey for Russian Jews was not easy. Jews were not allowed to leave Russia's Pale of Settlement, so they had to travel secretly.

Many young Jewish men walked miles across Europe. These men were called wayfarers or Fusgeyer. Wayfarers traveled from one Jewish community to the next selling goods to raise money for a boat ticket. Because they had no legal passports, wayfarers needed help from smugglers to cross borders into Germany, Austria, and Hungary. Some wayfarers were smuggled in carts of hay or potatoes.

Upon reaching the seaport, immigrants were examined by health inspectors. The health inspectors checked for signs of contagious diseases such as smallpox, typhus, and cholera. Infected people were not allowed on the boat.

Most Jewish immigrants traveled in the lower section of the ship called the steerage section. Immigrants traveled in steerage because it was all they could afford. Conditions were crowded. Passengers slept close together in narrow bunks. There was only one bathroom for hundreds of passengers. Diseases spread quickly.

The meals served on the ships were a problem for Jews. They could not eat much of the food because it was not prepared according to kosher laws. Instead of eating the food served on the ship, Jews ate the bread and tea they had brought with them.

Despite these uncomfortable conditions, Jewish immigrants passed the time by playing card games or listening to musicians. Others studied English so they would be able to understand the language of their new country.

# ★ Poppy Seed Cookies ★

Many Jewish immigrants prepared for the long trip to America by baking cookies and cakes. They brought these foods with them because the steamships did not serve kosher food.

## What You Need

### Ingredients:

$^1/_2$ cup (125 mL) butter

1 cup (250 mL) light brown sugar

2 eggs

1 $^1/_2$ teaspoons (7 mL) vanilla extract

1 cup (250 mL) flour

$^1/_2$ cup (125 mL) wheat germ

2 teaspoons (10 mL) baking powder

$^1/_2$ teaspoon (2 mL) salt

3 tablespoons (45 mL) poppy seeds

### Equipment:

baking sheet

parchment paper

electric mixer

large mixing bowl

dry-ingredient measuring cups

measuring spoons

two small spoons

pot holders

metal spatula

wire cooling rack

## What You Do

1. Preheat oven to 350°F (180°C).

2. Line baking sheet with parchment paper. Set aside.

3. With electric mixer, beat butter and light brown sugar in large mixing bowl until mixture is smooth.

4. Add eggs and vanilla and mix well.

5. Mix in flour, wheat germ, baking powder, and salt.

6. Mix poppy seeds into the mixture.

7. Lift a spoonful of dough with one spoon. With the other spoon, push dough off onto the parchment-lined baking sheet. Leave at least 2 inches (5 centimeters) of space between pieces of dough.

8. Bake 8 to 12 minutes until cookies are golden brown.

9. With pot holders, remove baking sheet from oven.

10. Use a metal spatula to move cookies onto a wire rack to cool.

*Makes about 2 dozen cookies*   15

# ARRIVING IN AMERICA

**B**etween 1855 and 1892, most Jewish immigrants arriving in New York passed through Castle Garden. This former fort was located on an island near lower Manhattan in New York. In 1892, the doors of Castle Garden closed because it was too small to handle the increasing number of immigrants. Jewish immigrants were soon directed to Ellis Island, another island located outside of Manhattan. Ellis Island opened to serve as a station to process large numbers of immigrants.

Each immigrant who passed through Ellis Island received a number. Health inspectors checked the immigrants for diseases and mental illness. Immigrants who failed the health inspection boarded ships back to the port where they had started.

Immigrants often spent an entire day passing through the long lines at Ellis Island. Inspectors had trouble keeping up with the huge numbers of immigrants. Some immigrants waited for many days on their ship before they could pass through the inspection lines on Ellis Island. Once they cleared Ellis Island, immigrants began to find their way in America.

Many German Jews had little or no money, so they traveled as peddlers. Jewish peddlers traveled with donkeys and horse-drawn wagons. Americans

*These Jewish men waited on their ship for their turn to pass through Ellis Island. This photograph was taken around 1920.*

generally welcomed German Jewish peddlers because they sold needed items such as cloth, tools, and clocks.

Some peddlers made enough money to open their own stores. They opened stores at a junction, a place where two roads meet. These Jewish businesses grew with the towns.

German Jewish immigrants settled in cities such as Chicago in Illinois, Cleveland in Ohio, and St. Louis in Missouri. Many huge department stores in America began as small Jewish businesses. Some of these stores include Macys, Bloomingdales, and Sears.

By 1880, many Jewish Americans found success as pharmacists, teachers, musicians, cigar makers, printers, bookbinders, and doctors.

While adapting to their new lives in America, many Jewish Americans became Reform Jews. These Jews gave up their old customs and laws. Reform Jews spoke English instead of Yiddish. They sent children to public schools instead of religious schools. Reform Jews wore modern clothing and stopped covering their heads with a skullcap, called a yarmulke, when they prayed. Men and women sat together in the synagogue. Not everyone obeyed strict kosher food laws.

Most Jewish immigrants from Russia and Poland stayed in the eastern United States. Many Jewish immigrants lived in New York City. Others settled in

*Many Jewish men earned their living as peddlers. They traveled from town to town selling goods such as tools and cloth.*

*To get away from the crowded living conditions in the tenement buildings, Jewish children often spent their time outdoors.*

large cities such as Baltimore in Maryland, and Philadelphia in Pennsylvania.

Jewish immigrants from Russia continued to wear their traditional clothing and spoke Yiddish or Hebrew. These differences caused many Americans to treat the Russian Jews unfairly. These Jews found it difficult to find housing because some Americans would not rent or sell to them. Others found it hard to find jobs. Many job ads posted in newspapers stated "Christians only."

In New York City, Jewish immigrants lived in tenement buildings. Many tenement apartments had only two or three rooms. Immigrants often ate, slept, washed clothes, and worked in the same room. Sometimes six people lived in a single room, and they had to take turns sleeping. Immigrants shared a bathroom with other families who lived on the same floor. It was not until 1901 that building codes required each apartment to have its own bathroom.

*Many Jewish immigrants lived in tenement buildings. Apartments in these buildings were crowded and uncomfortable.*

19

# SURVIVING IN AMERICA

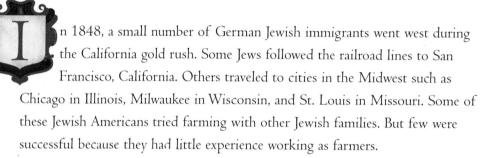

*Many immigrants went to work in garment shops. Immigrants worked many hours for very little pay.*

In 1848, a small number of German Jewish immigrants went west during the California gold rush. Some Jews followed the railroad lines to San Francisco, California. Others traveled to cities in the Midwest such as Chicago in Illinois, Milwaukee in Wisconsin, and St. Louis in Missouri. Some of these Jewish Americans tried farming with other Jewish families. But few were successful because they had little experience working as farmers.

Many Jewish immigrants used their tailoring skills to make clothing in New York's rapidly growing clothing industry. Some garment shops became known as sweatshops because the owners made employees work many hours in hot, poorly ventilated rooms.

Sweatshops were also noisy and dirty. Immigrants worked 16 hours a day and earned only $8 a week. Sometimes workers took piecework home to sew. Workers received payment for each piece of clothing they sewed. Children as young as 8 also worked in the shops to earn money for their families.

Jewish immigrants formed labor unions to help improve their working conditions.

*Members of the International Ladies Garment Workers' Union held strikes to force employers to improve their working conditions and wages in the clothing industry.*

Employees held strikes and refused to work until their working hours improved in the factories.

Jewish immigrants were among those who helped to create several important labor unions. In 1900, women formed the International Ladies Garment Workers' Union. Within the first two years, its members organized 189 strikes to demand higher wages and better working conditions. Samuel Gompers was a Jewish immigrant from England. He became president of another union called the American Federation of Labor.

Jewish immigrants also formed organizations to take care of each other. In 1843, they started the B'nai B'rith foundation. B'nai B'rith is Hebrew for "Sons of the Covenant." Today, it is the world's largest and oldest Jewish aid organization. Jewish immigrants began other groups including the Henry Street Settlement and the Educational Alliance in New York. In Chicago, they also founded the Hull House and the Hebrew Benevolent Society.

Jewish immigrants from the same shtetl in Russia or Europe formed groups in America called "landsmanshaftn."

*Eastern European Jewish men followed Jewish tradition by wearing dark clothing and long beards.*

By 1880, Jewish immigrants began to experience anti-Semitism. Many Eastern European Jewish men were easily identified by their dark clothes and long beards.

Some universities and medical schools secretly limited the number of Jews allowed into their schools. Religious tests in several states also barred Jews from some rights of citizenship. Jews were unable to serve on juries or hold public offices.

Unable to gain employment with traditional jobs, some Jews turned to new professions such as entertainment. The Yiddish Theater on the Lower East Side of New York City attracted many children to the theater and traveling shows. Later, many Jewish people became actors and entertainers in the movies, theater, radio, and on TV.

Many Jewish Americans became business leaders. They founded hospitals and schools. These Jewish institutions observed Jewish laws and had Yiddish-speaking doctors. By 1910, nearly every Jewish neighborhood in New York City had its own Jewish hospital.

Jewish immigrants found ways to have fun and keep their religious traditions. Jewish communities featured candy stores, delicatessens, soda fountains, and dance halls. Religion was still an important part of the Jewish life. Jewish immigrants built synagogues in tenement basements or in storefronts.

These social groups met to compare experiences and talk about life in the old country.

Landsmanshaftn members raised money for the sick and needy. Members helped each other find jobs, get medical care, and pay for funeral services for Jewish immigrants who had died in America. They also established new synagogues, political groups, labor unions, and schools.

*Jewish immigrants established synagogues in storefronts. Despite the unusual surroundings,*
*many Jewish immigrants continued to practice their faith.*

# KEEPING TRADITIONS

*Hanukkah is a holiday many Jewish Americans celebrate. The lighting of the menorah is part of the festivities.*

ewish immigrants have made many contributions to America. They passed their values of education, hard work, family, and religion down to younger generations. Today, these values are celebrated in Jewish holidays.

Rosh Hashanah, the Jewish New Year, begins the High Holy Days. During this 10-day festival, Jews ask God's forgiveness for their mistakes of the past year. The holiday occurs in fall and ends on Yom Kippur, the Jewish Day of Atonement.

Hanukkah is an eight-day holiday in December when people remember the ancient Jews' victory over a Syrian king. According to Jewish legend, when warriors entered the temple to claim victory, they found only enough oil to last one day. Their candles and candleholder, called a menorah, miraculously stayed lit for eight days. This time was long enough for them to get a new supply of oil.

Passover is an eight-day celebration that remembers the Jewish ancestors who fled from

# ★ Make a Dreidel ★

One of the best known symbols of Hanukkah is the dreidel. A dreidel is a four-sided top with a Hebrew letter on each side. The four letters mean "A Great Miracle Happened Here":

# נ ג ה ש

Players sit in a circle around a small bucket or bowl that serves as the pot. Each player (as well as the pot) begins with the same number of tokens. Use pennies, nuts, or raisins for tokens.

Players take turns spinning the dreidel. Whatever symbol faces up when the dreidel stops spinning tells the player what to do.

נ NUN - nothing happens; the next player spins the dreidel.
ג GIMEL - the player takes all tokens in the pot.
ה HEY - the player takes half the tokens in the pot.
ש SHIN - the player must put one token into the pot.

You can make a simple dreidel with a wooden dowel and a cube of Styrofoam.

## What You Need

pencil-size dowel, about 7 inches (18 centimeters) long
pencil sharpener

3-inch (7.5-centimeter) cube of Styrofoam
glue
paper

pencil
marking pen

## What You Do

1. Place one end of the dowel into a pencil sharpener and sharpen it to a point.

2. Place the pointed end of the dowel in the center of one side of the cube and push straight down.

3. Position the cube so that it is on the lower end of the dowel. Glue the dowel in place.

4. With paper and pencil, trace each of the four dreidel symbols. Use a marking pen to make the symbols easy to read.

5. Use scissors to cut a square around each symbol.

6. Glue one symbol on each of the four sides of the cube.

25

*Jewish Americans continue to follow their faith. Older generations pass down the traditions and rituals to younger generations.*

slavery in Egypt to freedom in Israel. Jewish families celebrate with meals, prayers, stories, and songs. The story is told during a festive meal called a seder.

Along with continuing their ancient religious rites and celebrations, Jewish Americans enjoyed lighter pastimes such as entertainment. Louis B. Mayer and Samuel Goldwyn were Jewish immigrants who created MGM Studios.

Today, the list of famous Jewish entertainers is long. Famous Jewish entertainers include Jerry Seinfeld, Barbra Streisand, Billy Crystal, Billy Joel, and Steven Spielberg.

Jews have made important contributions to medicine and science. Jonas Salk created the vaccine for polio, a disease that paralyzed children and adults during the 1940s and 1950s.

Albert Einstein was another Jewish scientist whose discoveries made major advances in science possible. Einstein discovered the theory of relativity. He also found that huge amounts of energy could be released when the atom is split. This knowledge contributed to the development of the atomic bomb.

Many Jewish foods have also become part of American life, including bagels. Today, many Americans enjoy delicatessen sandwiches, such as corned beef or pastrami on rye. Food companies that were started by Jewish Americans include Sara Lee and Häagen Daz.

# ★ Make a Family Tree ★

Genealogy is the study of family history. Genealogists often record this history in the form of a family tree. This chart records a person's ancestors, such as parents, grandparents, and great-grandparents.

Start your own family tree with the names of your parents and grandparents. Ask family members for their full names, including their middle names. Remember that your mother and grandmothers likely had a different last name before they were married. This name, called a maiden name, probably is the same as their fathers' last name.

Making a family tree helps you to know your ancestors and the countries from which they emigrated. Some people include the dates and places of birth with each name on their family tree. Knowing when and where these relatives were born will help you understand from which immigrant groups you have descended.

There are many ways to find information for your family tree. Ask for information from your parents, grandparents, and as many other older members of your family as you can. Some people research official birth and death records to find the full names of relatives. Genealogical societies often have information that will help with family tree research. If you know the cemetery where family members are buried, you may find some of the information you need on the gravestones.

Your father's mother

Your father's father

Your mother's father

Your mother's mother

Your father

Your mother

You

# ★ TIMELINE ★

**1654**

Jews come to America from Brazil, starting the first permanent settlement in what later became New York City.

**1820–1880**

The first wave of Jewish immigrants comes from Germany, Austria, and Hungary.

**1880–1920**

The second wave of Jewish immigrants comes from Poland, Russia and Romania, and other eastern European countries.

**1916**

Louis D. Brandei is the first Jewish person named as Supreme Court Justice.

**1941**

United States enters World War II. By the end of the war, 6 million Jews are killed in the Holocaust.

## 1600    1700    1800    1900

**1790**

Russia sets up the Pale of Settlement.

**1843**

Jewish immigrants found the B'nai B'rith.

**1881**

Jews create the Hebrew Immigrant Aid Society.

**1924**

The U.S. Congress limits the number of Jewish immigrants allowed entry into the United States.

**1948**

Israel becomes a homeland for Jews.

⭐ **Samuel Goldwyn** (1882–1974) Goldwyn was born in Warsaw, Poland. He traveled to the United States at age 13. In 1913, Goldwyn went into the film business. He became one of America's first motion picture producers. Goldwyn also helped to create MGM Studios, which produced many movies including *The Wizard of Oz*.

⭐ **Lenny Krayzelburg** (1975– ) An Olympic gold medalist, Krayzelburg was born in Odessa, Ukraine. He immigrated to the United States with his parents in 1989. He became a U.S. citizen in 1995. Krayzelburg won three gold medals in swimming at the 2000 Olympic Games.

*Lenny Krayzelburg*

⭐ **Joseph Pulitzer** (1847–1911) Born in Budapest, Hungary, Pulitzer came to America in 1864. He fought in the Civil War (1861–1865) and later became a journalist. After his death, the Pulitzer Prize in literature was created in his honor.

⭐ **Steven Spielberg** (1946– ) Spielberg was born in Cincinnati, Ohio. He began making movies as a teenager. Today, Spielberg is both a motion picture director and a producer. Some of his movies include *Jaws*, *E.T.–The Extra-Terrestrial*, *Jurassic Park*, *Back to the Future*, *Schindler's List*, and *Saving Private Ryan*.

⭐ **Barbra Streisand** (1942– ) Streisand was born in Brooklyn, New York. She is a singer, actress, producer, and director. Streisand starred in several movies including *Hello Dolly!*, *What's Up, Doc?*, *The Way We Were*, and *The Mirror Has Two Faces*. In 1983, Streisand starred in the movie *Yentl*. She became the first woman to co-write, produce, direct, and star in a movie.

*Barbra Streisand*

# Words to Know

**anti-Semitism** (an-tee-SEM-e-tiz-um)—social discrimination against Jews and Judaism

**cobbler** (KOB-lur)—someone who makes or repairs shoes

**Holocaust** (HOL-uh-kost)—the killing of millions of European Jews and others by the Nazis during World War II (1939–1945)

**kosher** (KOH-shur)—food prepared or eaten according to Jewish laws

**menorah** (muh-NOR-uh)—candleholder with seven or nine candles; menorahs are used in Jewish religious ceremonies.

**pogrom** (PO-grem)—act of violence against Jewish people in the Pale of Settlement, the area where Jews were forced to live in Russia

**seder** (SAY-der)—traditional Passover meal

**shtetl** (SHTET-el)—a small village or town

**tsar** (ZAR)—an emperor of Russia before the revolution of 1917

**Yiddish** (YID-ish)—language that combines Hebrew and German, written in the Hebrew alphabet

# To Learn More

Frost, Helen. *German Immigrants, 1820-1920*. Coming to America. Mankato, Minn.: Blue Earth Books, 2002.

Horton, Casey. *The Jews*. We Came to North America. New York: Crabtree Publishing, 2000.

Leder, Jane Mersky. *A Russian Jewish Family*. Journey between Two Worlds. Minneapolis: Lerner Publications, 1996.

Wallner, Rosemary. *Polish Immigrants, 1890-1920*. Coming to America. Mankato, Minn.: Blue Earth Books, 2003.

Weitzman, Elizabeth. *I Am Jewish American*. Our American Family. New York: PowerKids Press, 1997.

# Places to Write and Visit

American Jewish Historical Society
15 West 16th Street
New York, NY 10011

The Jewish Museum
1109 Fifth Avenue at 92nd Street
New York, NY 10128

National Museum of American Jewish History
Independence Mall East
55 North Fifth Street
Philadelphia, PA 19106-2197

Skirball Cultural Center
2701 North Sepulveda Boulevard
Los Angeles, CA 90049

United States Holocaust Memorial Museum
100 Raoul Wallenberg Place, SW
Washington, DC 20024-2126

# Internet Sites

American Jewish Historical Society
http://www.ajhs.org

Builders of America - "The Jewish Heritage"
http://www.borisamericanjews.org

Jewish American Hall of Fame
http://amuseum.org/jahf

Lower East Side Tenement Museum
http://www.tenement.org

National Museum of American Jewish History
http://nmajh.org

United States Holocaust Memorial Museum
http://www.ushmm.org

# Index

anti-Semitism, 9–10, 11, 18, 22

Castle Garden, 16

diseases, 14, 16, 26

Ellis Island, 16

garment shops, 20, 21

Hanukkah, 24, 25
Holocaust, 10, 11

inspections, 14, 16

labor unions, 20–21, 22

Pale of Settlement, 9–10, 14
Passover, 24, 26
peddlers, 10, 12, 16–17
piecework, 20
pogroms, 10
port cities, 5, 14

Reform Jews, 17

shtetls, 10, 21
steamships, 12, 15
steerage, 12, 14
synagogue, 8, 17, 22, 23

tailors, 10, 20
tenement buildings, 18, 19, 22

World War I, 11
World War II, 10, 11

Yiddish, 9, 17, 18, 22

## DATE DUE